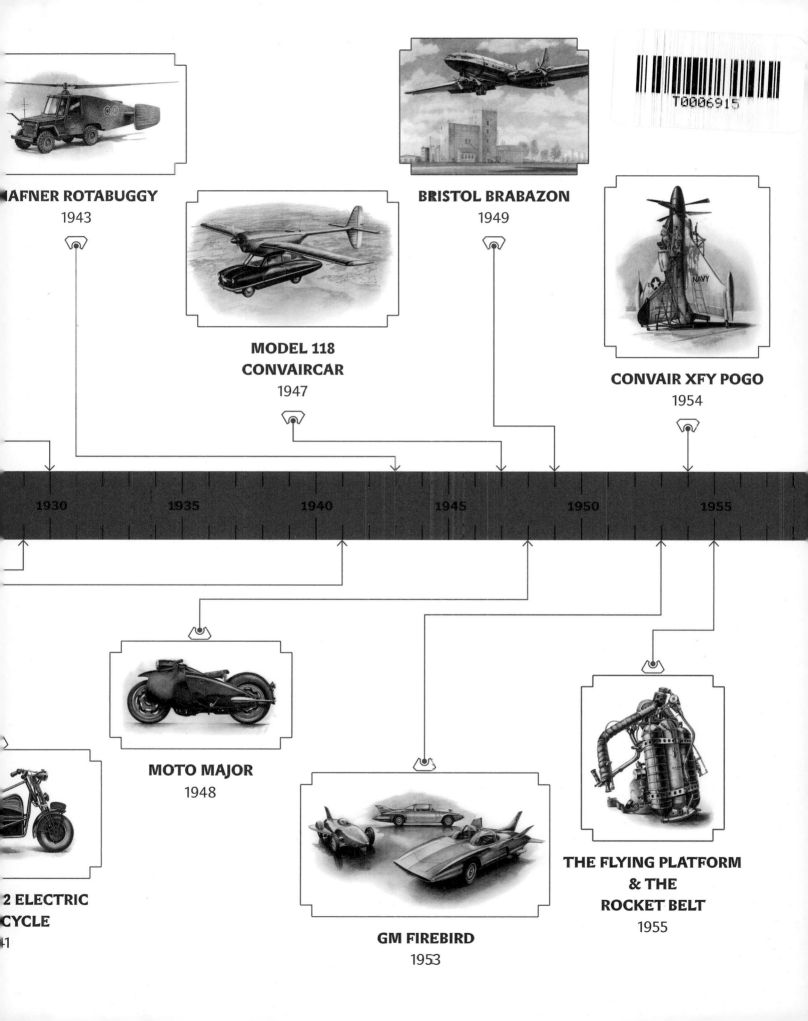

HAFNER ROTABUGGY
1943

BRISTOL BRABAZON
1949

MODEL 118
CONVAIRCAR
1947

CONVAIR XFY POGO
1954

MOTO MAJOR
1948

2 ELECTRIC
CYCLE
41

GM FIREBIRD
1953

THE FLYING PLATFORM
& THE
ROCKET BELT
1955

1930   1935   1940   1945   1950   1955

MEANS OF TRANSPORT
THAT *ALMOST* CHANGED
THE WORLD

Albatros

Dodge Deora—page 40

TABLE OF CONTENTS

INTRODUCTION

If a thing is known, it's usually because it's the largest, fastest, strongest, most expensive, or smallest around. It's easy to remember. People often talk about it or write books, shoot documentaries, or even award-winning movies about it. Everyone knows of these things, many of which are means of transport.

Some means of transport, though, aren't the best at something or featured in a movie, but they do play a role in our lives without us even realizing it. Buses, trains, ships, planes, cars that aren't record-holders but can be relied on. Every day they push our world forward, making sure it never stops moving.

And then there are the means of transport that people talk about once in a while and that sometimes appear in movies, documentaries, or books. But you never actually see them on the road, because either they never existed or they didn't prove their worth.

Take the remote-controlled car, for example. Perhaps you have a toy version at home you play with. But imagine what it would be like if your parents had a life-sized version. You'd sit in it and they'd use the remote control to drive you to school and back home again. If you think about it, there are many holes in this idea. In fact, it may be complete nonsense, but we definitely aren't the first to invent it. It has popped into many smart heads and been built by many skilled hands, though it has never been driven by everyday people.

In 1925, for example, one such car was presented to the public. Francis Houdina wanted to show off his invention, so the remote-controlled car set out into the streets. It looked to be driven by a ghost and scared the onlookers. And unfortunately, they remained scared because the car headed straight for them, causing quite a stir in the streets of New York City. Francis Houdina

was advised to never try anything like this ever again. Also, the famous escape artist Harry Houdini, having caught wind of the accident, got angry because the company's name resembled his and smashed up the inventor's office. Which is strange, considering

A Chandler 1926 model by the Chandler Motor Car Company, this one equipped by Francis Houdina with a radio antenna to enable remote control.

the illusionist himself borrowed the name from the magician Jean Eugène Robert-Houdin. Some claim that none of it mattered, though, and that the argument was staged as a marketing gimmick to draw attention away from the panic the cars had caused.

Surely this is the first time you've heard this story. Some things and people are unfortunately described as average, forgotten, useless, expensive, or insignificant. And it's precisely these means of transport we're excited to tell you about.

MOVING WALKWAY

S tand still and let yourself be moved around by the pavement to the other side of the city—and then back again. Your feet don't hurt. You're nice and comfortable. Free to admire the city around you. It's quite common today and you can stumble upon moving walkways at just about any airport, but imagine it's way back in the year 1900! Both personal and public transport are metaphorically—thankfully—still in their diapers, and all of a sudden you're confronted with a moving walkway. Where? In Paris, of course! This grand convenience was installed there as part of a world's fair known as the Paris Exposition. Some relished in riding the pavement, seen by the era's engineers as the future of mass transport, while others were too afraid. Just imagine stepping off a platform and onto a moving belt, with no stops, and having to jump off again. And what if you wore a long skirt or elegant suit? At first you'd need to jump onto a slower walkway that moved at 2.5 miles per hour, and after that onto the faster one, which raced along at an astonishing 5 miles per hour. Those who, trembling with fear, clung to posts, while the braver ones further increased their speed by walking forward. Groundbreaking and entertaining as it was, though, the joy of riding through Paris on a moving walkway could be enjoyed only in the first year of the 20th century.

> Moving walkways were put to use much later, for example in department stores and at airports.

BRENNAN'S MONORAIL

Get ready for something that will blow your mind. It's entirely common—and by now not exactly noteworthy—that trains use two rails, but have you ever heard of a single-rail train?

Once upon a time it seemed like the greatest idea in the world. Engineers began thinking about developing a fast one-wheel train that could quickly negotiate turns, and they even set about actually making it. If you dislike two-wheel designs—say, if you took a bad fall from your bicycle—well then, rest assured that the gyro monorail, as such trains are known, could straighten up after tilting. And it could remain straight and safe even with a single wheel, thanks to something called the gyroscope—an invention designed to keep the train upright.

In fact, the design was being independently perfected by two engineers whose creations went on to delight the hearts of those lucky few who rode them. One of the best-known prototypes—Brennan's Monorail—inspired much more modern projects, also based on the idea of a single-rail train.

As you may have noticed, despite their obvious advantages, gyro monorails—unlike the typical double-rail train—aren't exactly common. Why? Money. Gyroscopes were just too expensive to be put into regular use. Moreover, many tracks would have needed to undergo costly, complex reconstruction. After all, they were originally built to serve traditional trains. But don't throw in the towel just yet! The gyro monorail's time might still come—perhaps in the far future . . . For now, the whole idea seems too crazy.

What is a gyroscope?
The gyro monorail's mysterious energy came from it being balanced by two spinning wheels—called gyroscopes—mounted side by side, spinning in opposite directions. This was how it overcame the instability of balancing on top of a single rail.

RMS *OLYMPIC*

For many European families a century ago, transoceanic voyages were an opportunity for a better future, a way to leave behind their crisis-ridden countries for the land of opportunity—the United States. The three ships of the shipping company White Star Line could also be seen as a family.

The most famous one was the *Titanic*, whose end was historically tragic. Even the *Titanic*'s younger sister, the *Brittanic*, ended tragically. It was originally named the *Gigantic*, after the race from Greek mythology, but its new name didn't bring it much luck. The *Brittanic* wasn't a luxury transoceanic ship but a floating military hospital. World War I changed many plans and lives, and the ship met her match in the form of a naval mine.

But the oldest and least-known member was the steamship *Olympic*, which was ever-so-slightly smaller than the *Titanic*, although it also didn't escape the family curse. During its fifth voyage, it crashed into the cruiser HMS *Hawk*. Since the crash was the *Olympic*'s fault, this had a negative effect on the White Star Line's finances. Just like her younger sister, the *Olympic* had to join the war. She survived and even managed to sink a German submarine, saving the lives of 9,000 U.S. soldiers. Unfortunately, the postwar era brought the ship no glory, and in 1935 she was sold for part. You can encounter fragments of her interior displayed in British restaurants and hotels. And so ends the story of these three nautical sisters.

During the war, the ship's design was adjusted so that it would be difficult to tell how far away it was and at what speed it was moving, thereby making it harder to hit.

JUNKERS J1000

The plane was huge even by today's standards. By comparison, the wingspan of the famous Boeing 747 is actually 8 inches shorter.

Hugo Junkers (1859–1935), a famous German engineer, aircraft designer, and entrepreneur, wanted to develop a special transatlantic airplane for flights to the United States. He'd already designed the world's first all-metal plane—the Junkers F13—so why shouldn't he succeed in making a huge transatlantic plane? He sat down at his desk to draw, calculate, and design, and with the help of his head engineer, Otto Mader, invented a truly futuristic machine—one with a double fuselage connected by a pair of robust wings.

The main wing was huge enough to fit cabins and even bedrooms for 80 to 100 passengers and 10 crewmembers—12 cabins for six people and 14 cabins for two people. The seats were designed to make them easy to turn into beds. Hugo Junkers expected the incredible aircraft to spend up to ten straight hours in the air without landing, which made comfort very important. The main wing also contained a generously spaced hold. The fuselages functioned as a dining room and a lookout area. This plane of the future had four engines and retractable landing gear.

Hugo Junkers's design was ahead of its time by several decades. As tends to be the case with groundbreaking inventions, however, it was not fully appreciated at the time. American investors weren't interested in the Junkers J1000, and so the transatlantic project was never implemented, though some of its design features were later incorporated into other planes.

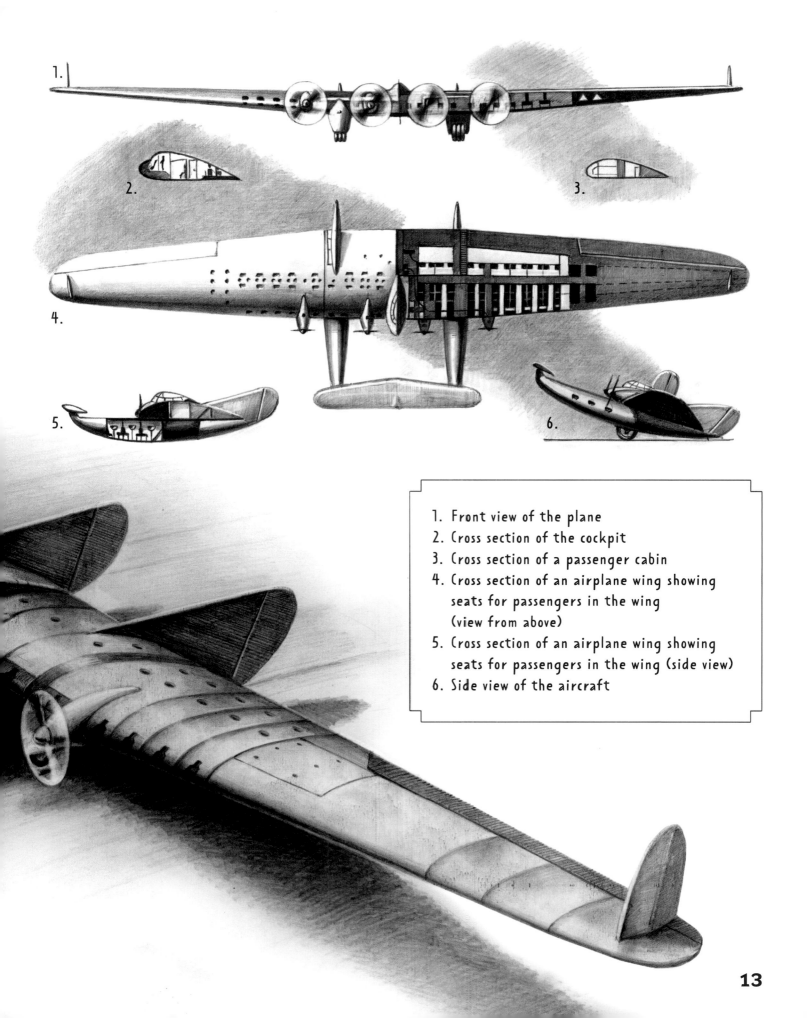

1. Front view of the plane
2. Cross section of the cockpit
3. Cross section of a passenger cabin
4. Cross section of an airplane wing showing
   seats for passengers in the wing
   (view from above)
5. Cross section of an airplane wing showing
   seats for passengers in the wing (side view)
6. Side view of the aircraft

DORNIER DO X

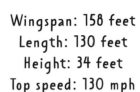

Wingspan: 158 feet
Length: 130 feet
Height: 34 feet
Top speed: 130 mph

"**W**hat is that monstrosity floating up there in the air?"

"An aircraft. I've never seen anything like it."

"No, it's not a plane, I don't think. It's a huge boat with wings."

These may have been the excited whispers exchanged in the early 20th century by those who watched the test flights of the Dornier Do X, a German flying boat. At the time, it was the world's largest and heaviest vessel, and its gigantic deck could accommodate nearly 100 passengers and 14 crewmembers. To make sure no one would get bored during the long journeys, the engineers gave their gigantic hydroplane some truly astonishing furnishings—three decks, bars, restaurants, and areas for gentlemen to enjoy an afternoon cigar. If you got too tired, you could simply tilt your seat back and turn it into a comfortable bed.

This heavenly giant was constructed in 1929 and soared up in the sky exactly 103 times. Eventually, it came to light that its engines were too weak to carry the boat's exceptional weight—over 30 tons with no passengers—plus they regularly overheated and could only lift the machine 1,400 feet above the surface. So the designers added more powerful motors, allowing the Dornier Do X to rise much higher and cross the Atlantic Ocean.

"Wonderful! Awesome! Amazing!"

Calm down, my friends. During a test flight over German cities, or rather while landing by a lake in the city of Passau, the gigantic boat suddenly lost its equally gigantic tail. And so ended the famous career of a luxury sky vessel that never really got off the ground.

The Dornier Do X arriving in New York City →

DYNASPHERE

"Help, there's a huge tire speeding down the road! Get out of the way or it will run us all over!"

Don't worry, though. This 10-foot, 1,000-pound wheel didn't break loose. Take a closer look and you'll see a driver sitting inside, in full control of everything. It was the 1930s and the budding car industry was on the cusp of booming. Truly, it was the best time to give many different ideas a try, including a prototype by the British electrical engineer John Archibald Purves, who, inspired by the drawings of the genius Renaissance inventor Leonardo da Vinci, created a bizarre so-called Dynasphere, nicknamed Jumbo. This unusual tire-shaped vehicle with 10 metal rings arranged next to one another was believed to have a bright future ahead, in part because the moving metal structure could maintain a significant amount of power with limited engine use. But the Jumbo had one jumbo-sized disadvantage: its low speed. You couldn't get very far at 30 miles per hour. The complicated controls didn't make the monowheel popular either. The driver sat on a small seat inside the wheel, pressing on pedals with their feet to change gears and go into reverse. The only way to negotiate a turn, though, was to lean in the direction you wanted to go. Not exactly comfortable, right? And so, although Archibald Purves made two types of the Jumbo—one running on petrol and the other on diesel—and although he did all he could to fine-tune these unique vehicles, the Dynasphere never made it in the car industry and is viewed today as a peculiar goof.

J. A. Purves's dynasphere, driven by Charles Eric Purves, the doctor's son.

The press called the Dynasphere the car of the future.

SOCOVEL 1942 ELECTRIC MOTORCYCLE

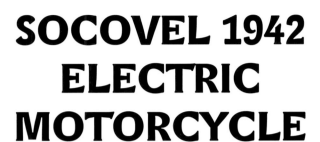

I t's said that every cloud has a silver lining, and sometimes that's true. Like in the case of Maurice Limelette, who was lying in a hospital, recovering from a serious car crash. Bored as he was, he had founded the Brussels Society for Studying and Constructing Electric Vehicles (Socovel) with his brother, and because his fascination with motor vehicles never left him, even after his terrifying encounter, he came up with a prototype of the electric motorcycle.

Since the world was being ravaged by war at the time—World War II, in fact, which led to gas shortages and rationing—electric vehicles were a way out of the mess. The design of an electricity-powered motorcycle immediately captured the attention of the Germans, who allowed the brothers to make 500 such motorcycles. The electric motorcycle was met with enthusiastic support from the general public. Although it was prohibitively expensive—the brothers bought their parts from different companies—400 of the bikes were sold in 1942.

But then the German army set its sight on them. The light bikes—with a top speed of 15 mph, a range of 30 miles, and 10 hours of charging time—would have been useful at airports as transport vehicles. The brothers didn't feel like collaborating with the occupiers and enemies of their country, so they refused to comply. Finally, peace came and with it enough gas. The enthusiasm for expensive electric motorcycles began dropping steadily. In the early 1950s, the Socovel company still had 80 military motorcycles left in its warehouse. But with nobody interested anymore, what were they to do with them? *Scrap them,* thought the brothers. And that's just what they did.

The motorbike's original design

The current, restored design

HAFNER ROTABUGGY

World War II lit a fire under engineers, designers, and scientists, motivating them to discover something new to help people survive those crazy times. With limited funding, they came up with timeless prototypes, one of them being the Hafner Rotabuggy—a flying jeep. British army engineers wanted this vehicle to be able to fly—yes, you read that correctly—just about anywhere if necessary, quickly and without wasting time. Upon arrival, soldiers were to use it like they would any other off-road vehicle. Once required somewhere else it'd spin its propeller and wheel, be off, and fly to another unit before the company could say anything.

This practical army hybrid was authored by Raul Hafner, a technician working for Britain's Royal Air Force who had already made a proposal for a single-seat glider. The Hafner Rotabuggy was based on the concept of a glider. In order to take off, it needed to reach its top speed, but as revealed by the first test, conducted on December 16, 1943, the test freight vehicle couldn't do that. On December 27, 1943, though, the test succeeded and a 4.5-liter-engine Bentley rose to the sky. Hurray!

Easy there. Once the vehicle reached 44 mph, its robust body began shaking uncontrollably, forcing the driver-pilot to land. But Raul Hafner didn't give up. He kept working on the Rotabuggy, kept perfecting the design. The final test flight took place on February 1, 1944, and was very successful. But . . . it was too late. There wasn't any interest in the flying jeep anymore. In the meantime, other smart engineers had developed gliders that could easily transport military vehicles to wherever they needed to go . . .

Raoul Hafner also proposed a "rotachute"—named after the parachute—to help soldiers land at the exact spot of their choosing. But it was never widely used.

MODEL 118 CONVAIRCAR

Imagine a car that's going about its business when suddenly there's a bad traffic jam up ahead, so the driver guns the accelerator and flies away!

"Futuristic?" you say. "Impossible?"

Quite the contrary. Enthusiastic car engineers have been trying to design such a multipurpose vehicle since the early 20th century. Some tried to attach wings to the car, while others invented planes whose wings would fold upon landing, allowing them to drive on roads. The postwar era, especially, had no shortage of such experiments. It was also then that two Americans, Theodore P. Hall and Tommy Thompson, introduced the Convair 116, a winged two-seated vehicle.

It was in 1946. After 66 test flights, they decided to perfect the design, since now they knew how to go about it. And so a year later the world was blessed with a fine-tuned, technologically perfected model: the Convair 118. Fans of planes and cars alike rubbed their hands together in anticipation. Everything suggested that the multipurpose vehicle would go into mass production.

Unfortunately, however, during the very first test flight, Theodore and Tommy had to perform an emergency landing. And the reason behind this unexpected failure?

A silly mistake. Although the car's fuel tank was full, as it should have been, the plane's was not . . . Unfortunately, the rescue maneuver damaged the vehicle quite a bit. Hall and Thompson got down to business, repaired their flying car, and turned it into another model. As it turned out, their efforts were in vain. By then, people had lost interest in combining driving and flying. And so the groundbreaking project was forgotten by pretty much everyone.

MOTO MAJOR

The motorcycle was designed
in the Art Deco style created
in the 1920s and widespread mostly
in the United States and Europe.

A motorcycle is a work of art? Nonsense. The point of motorbikes is for us to get from point A to point B, is it not? And to do it as fast as possible. But the Moto Major, designed by Italian engineer Salvatore Majorca, was a true work of art, a product that wasn't meant to just thunder through the streets but to earn people's admiration. The bike is completely covered with an elegant aerodynamic steel bodywork—except for the handlebars, seat, and wheels, naturally—which, along with shock absorbers shaped like fish tails, gives the vehicle a unique futuristic appearance.

The word *aerodynamic* is quite appropriate for the Moto Major. Majorca developed his vehicle in the aerodynamic research center of the Turin company Aeritalia, which also funded the whole project—and generously. In 1948, the exquisitely designed motorbike, powered by a two-cylinder liquid-cooled engine, took the breath away from anyone who attended the Salon of Milan, where the beauty was first presented to much fanfare. Although the bike amazed everyone who saw it, it never went into production and remained a prototype, as well as a dream of enthusiastic bikers who kept wondering what the world of motoring would have looked like had the perfect Moto Major been given the thumbs-up. Perhaps completely, utterly different.

A single prototype remains in its original,
non-renovated condition.

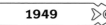

BRISTOL BRABAZON

It's the dawn of the 1940s. The world is being ravaged by World War II, but clever minds are already wondering what will happen once it ends. Specifically, about air transport and the direction it would take. This is why Britain's so-called Brabazon Committee was established in 1942, presided over by Lord Brabazon, the first Englishman to ever pilot a heavier-than-air aircraft.

And so, as the war raged on, engineers and technicians began developing a plane that would, in peacetime, transport passengers far beyond the Atlantic Ocean. It was just as ambitious of a project as the one by Hugo Junkers in 1929, if you'll recall. So, the Bristol aviation company adjusted its model of a long-range eight-engine bomber, entered the competition, and won. The Brabazon Committee required that Bristol make two prototypes of a comfortable long-range airliner for at least 100 passengers and 8 crewmembers. The committee particularly stressed the need for a robust fuselage so that each passenger would have enough space, as though they were sitting alone in a personal car. The wealthier ones were even to enjoy the space equivalent to two personal cars. The twelve-hour flights

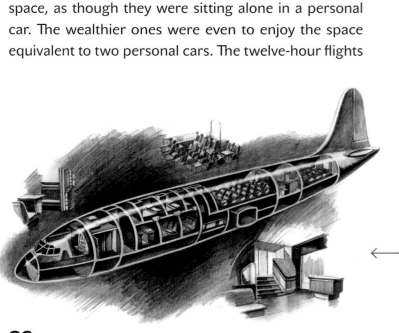

The luxurious cabin was supposed to accommodate up to 100 passengers.

were to be made more palatable by a movie theater, lounge, and bar serving refreshments. Wonderful, right?

It would have been even more wonderful if the construction of this monstrous aircraft had begun in a better time and suited the tastes of the investors. The Brabazon Committee somehow overlooked that airline carriers back then were interested in fast, economical planes. What good would such a slow, luxurious giant be? And so in 1953, the only Bristol Brabazon ever produced was broken up for scrap. By then, it had 382 test flight hours under its belt, without a single paying passenger on board.

GM FIREBIRD

GM Firebird I

As you've surely noticed, this book covers several attempts at combining different types of public transport. Seaplanes, flying cars, rotor aircraft—all these peculiar vehicles wanted to fly and ride, fly and float, or fly and fly at the same time. Unfortunately, however, none of them became a hit in the field of transportation, though not for a lack of trying. Isn't that sad? Imagine being able to drive for a while and then take off once you get bored with the road, or slide down onto a river and ride its waves while those driving regular cars are going insane in endless traffic jams.

This story of four cars resembling jets or spacecraft is a bit different. They never yearned for the spotlight, which may be why, unlike other examples, they never knew the bitter taste of defeat.

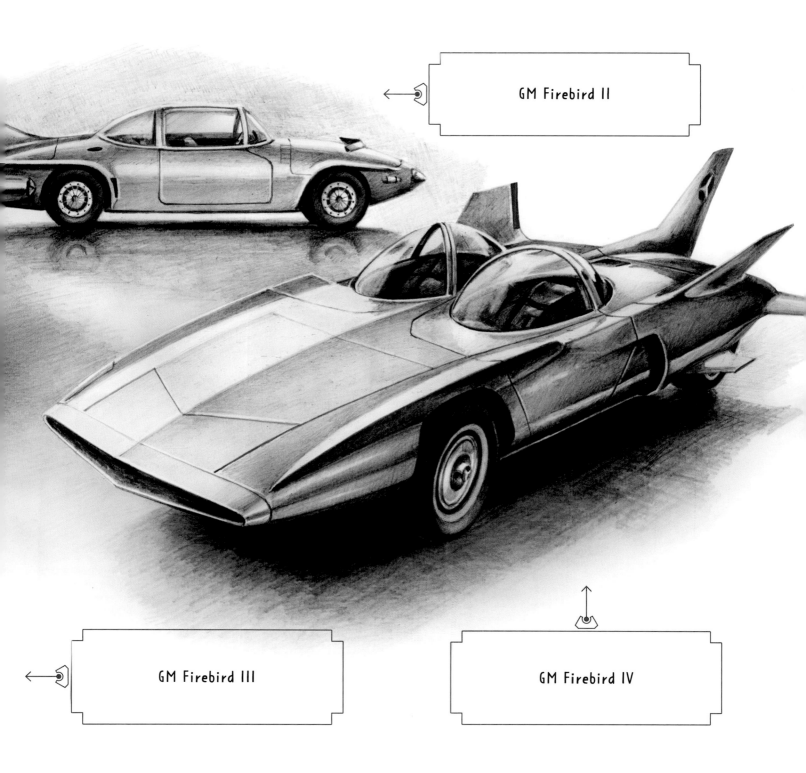

GM Firebird II

GM Firebird III

GM Firebird IV

The Firebird series by General Motors was created in the 1950s simply to showcase technological development—by attaching wheels to rockets! They're made from titanium and have air drag brakes, similar to those found in airplanes. And they definitely needed them. If this fully air-conditioned luxury car had gone into serial production, the roads would have been full of cars driving at nearly 200 miles per hour. But because nobody at General Motors was interested in that, these vehicles simply appear like a *Design for Dreaming*. Incidentally, that's the name of a short film featuring the Firebird II. Look it up online and imagine what the world would have looked like if the dream had come true.

CONVAIR XFY POGO

The 1950s. Shortly after the devastating Second World War, the world is once again engulfed in war, this time a cold one. Two enemy camps: the communist East against the democratic West. Both sides are arming themselves in case the Cold War turns into an actual open conflict. The powers have to be prepared, which is why they're attempting to make the impossible.

Namely, a plane that can take off from an incredibly small area. A plane capable of standing on its tail, taking off vertically, and only assuming the horizontal position once safely in the sky. Naturally, it would also land vertically. "That's it!" rejoiced U.S. engineers, who set about constructing the amazing VTOL (Vertical Take-Off and Landing) machine. There was only one problem, though. In order for the aircraft to take off vertically, it needed to be equipped with ultra-strong engines with a thrust much greater than the weight of the entire machine.

But the engineers refused to let this obstacle deter them. They fitted the aircraft with a powerful turboprop engine and got down to business. The prototype of this devilish machine first took off in 1954. It rose vertically and then elegantly tipped itself to the standard horizontal position.

But what about it taking too long? What about the plane being too difficult to control? No problem—air force pilots are the best of the best. What the engineers didn't count on, however, was a certain level of discomfort during landing. Pilots really struggled with positioning the plane vertically while carefully throttling back and looking over their shoulder—it was just too much! And so, this breakthrough project never saw the light of day. Two years later, in 1956, the Convair XFY Pogo was discontinued. Who would waste time on such an impractical machine, right?

THE FLYING PLATFORM & THE ROCKET BELT

Quick! Plug your ears or you'll go deaf! Hear that roaring? You can't miss it! That's because there's a propeler-powered platform flying directly above our heads and in the middle there stands, incredibly, a man. "Hey there, hold on so that you don't fall off and break your bones!"

The flying platform prototype was developed in the 1950s to fulfill the needs of the U.S. Army. The military was looking for ways to safely cross, for example, minefields. So Charles H. Zimmerman, at a Californian workshop called Hiller, came up with the Hiller VZ-1 Pawnee. The platform had many benefits, but also some

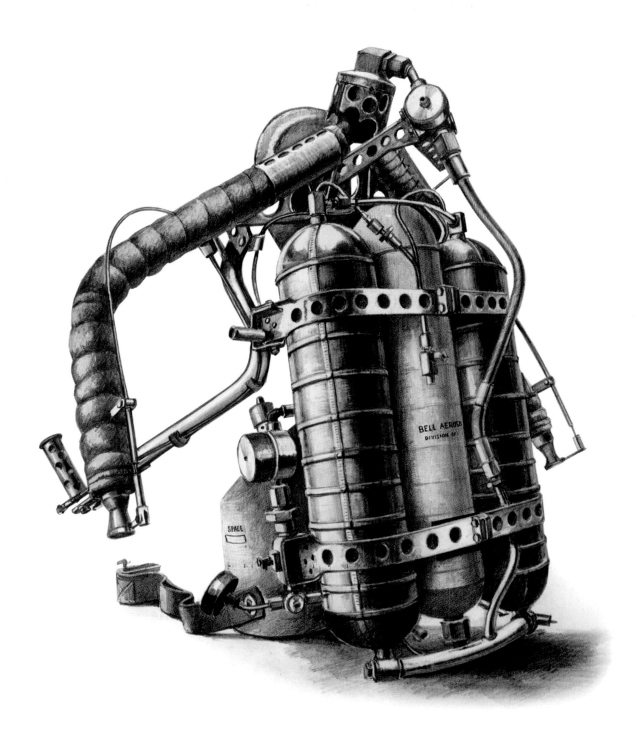

drawbacks, one of them being the deafening noise, as well as the low speed and high instability. In the end, Zimmermann didn't live long enough to see his Hiller VZ–1 Pawnee implemented. But who wouldn't like to fly like a bird? Imagine an entire flying army soaring high above.

This may have been the idea behind another plan the army concocted. This gadget saw the light of day in the 1960s. But what exactly was it? A backpack with a fuel tank and an engine that made its wearer fly. Not only was the device hard to keep stable—an almost inhuman task when you're high in the air—but the maximum flight time was a mere 30 seconds. Considering the danger, it's no wonder that this seemingly wonderful invention never made a mark on the world and is remembered only as a funny—and pretty crazy!—experiment.

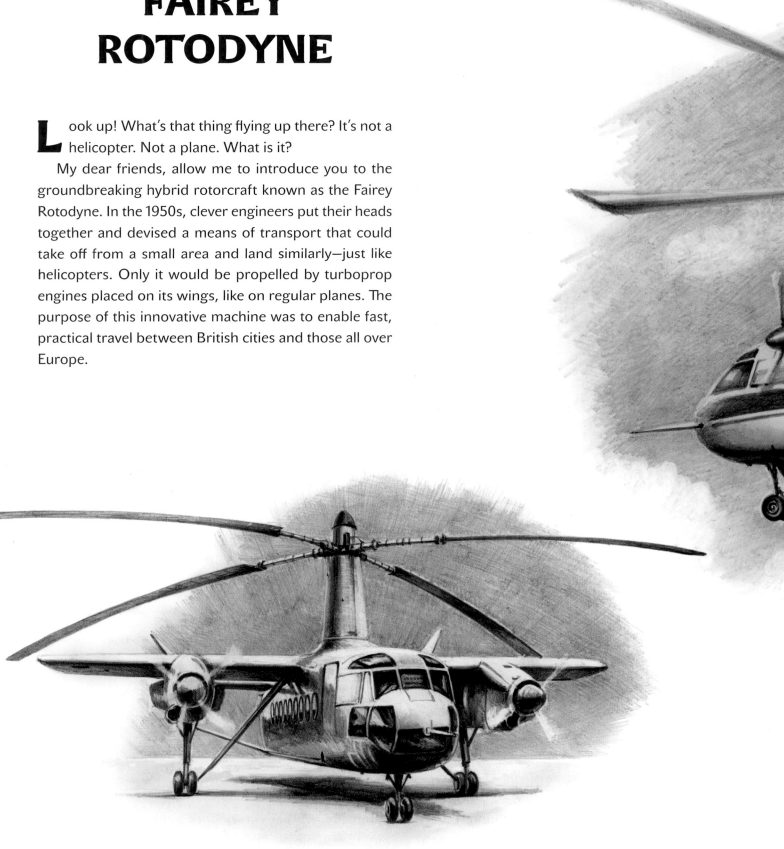

FAIREY ROTODYNE

Look up! What's that thing flying up there? It's not a helicopter. Not a plane. What is it?

My dear friends, allow me to introduce you to the groundbreaking hybrid rotorcraft known as the Fairey Rotodyne. In the 1950s, clever engineers put their heads together and devised a means of transport that could take off from a small area and land similarly—just like helicopters. Only it would be propelled by turboprop engines placed on its wings, like on regular planes. The purpose of this innovative machine was to enable fast, practical travel between British cities and those all over Europe.

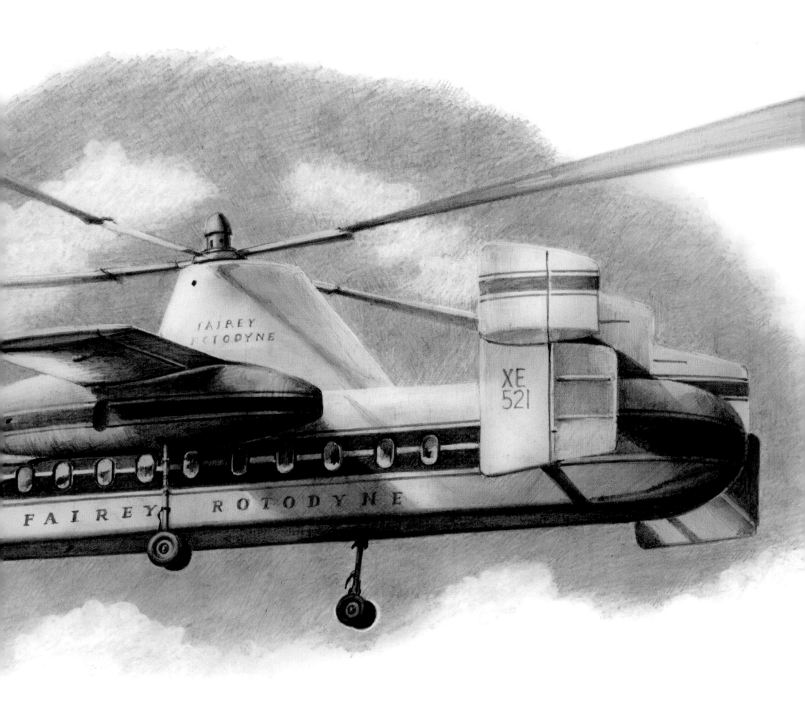

The British government had high hopes for this project and planned for the Fairey Rotodynes to take over large chunks of public transport. Maybe there'd come a time when people would turn their noses up at sluggish trains and ferries, instead getting on a Fairey Rotodyne and arriving in their destination before they'd finish reading their favorite magazine. Unfortunately, this promising vision encountered an unpromising problem. When the Fairey was taking off and landing, its jets gave an incredibly loud rumble, making people wonder where it could even operate. Definitely not in built-up areas—the locals would go crazy.

So how did it end? Badly. In 1962, the British government gave up on the project and scrapped the Rotodyne. Thus ended 12 long years of development on an aircraft that was neither a plane nor a chopper but was unimaginably loud.

AVRO CANADA VZ-9 AV AVROCAR

What's that weird object up in the sky? A flying saucer?! A real, actual flying saucer?! Could it be that aliens have finally decided to visit us here on Earth?

Not at all, in fact. It's the 1950s and this futuristic object, which has always been associated with extra-terrestrial civilizations, is being operated by a person, a mere mortal. Specifically, by a single pilot, even though the side cockpit and the whole control room were designed to fit two crewmembers. The ultra-modern aircraft, made by a Canadian firm and operated with a single control lever, was pushed into production by the Cold War, a silent conflict between Eastern and

The press nicknamed it the "flying jeep."

Western powers that came very, very close to ending in a catastrophic nuclear war. And so the arms race was on, and both sides were engaged in developing and constructing weapons. The Avrocar flying saucer was to become a new type of fighter plane and fly at supersonic speeds, at incredible altitudes. It wouldn't need a runway, since it would be able to take off from a small area and land there again, just like a helicopter. In fact, the engineers believed the Avrocar would come to replace helicopters. The aircraft's shape was inspired by the Frisbee, adopting the curved upper part of the popular children's toy.

The development began in 1952. Seven years later, the saucer took flight for the first time—or at least tried to. In 1961, the ambitious project was discontinued and canceled. The flying objects, which would have been at home in any sci-fi movie about first contact, never made the Earth's sky their home.

NS *SAVANNAH*

The first ever steamship to conquer the Atlantic Ocean—way back in 1818—used the SS abbreviation before its name, for "steamship." The SS *Savannah* could be viewed as the great-grandmother to the NS *Savannah*, which went to ocean 144 later, in 1962. Since then, many ships have crossed the ocean that separates America from Europe, but none of the others had the NS abbreviation as a part of its name—meaning "nuclear ship."

The 1950s, just like the whole of modern society, were profoundly shaped by atomic explosions. The nuclear bomb, a devastating weapon, demonstrated the power of science and mankind and ended World War II. The fear of it being dropped again forced the world to maintain peace. President Eisenhower even decided to launch the Atoms for Peace project to showcase the positive power of nuclear energy. And it was this beneficial project that created the granddaughter to the famous *Savannah* steamboat.

The ship was supposed to be the first one in history to use nuclear propulsion for non-military purposes. The luxury merchant ship, with fully air-conditioned cabins and swimming pools, took their passengers on voyages to the future, which made it comparable to not only her direct ancestor, but also to the *Titanic*, her distant cousin, whose fate was sealed by an ordinary iceberg. The fate of the NS *Savannah*, however, was determined by financial issues. Revenues over her 10-year career amounted to a mere $12 million, while the costs soared to nearly $50 million. It was suggested that the luxury boat be turned into a floating power station, but in the end it became a museum and reminder of the ideals of nuclear peace.

Length: 600 feet
Draft: 80 feet
Top speed: 27 mph
Capacity: 60 passengers
+ 14,040 tons of cargo

The ship's control room, where engineers controlled the reactor and steam propulsion.

DODGE DEORA

There are no doors anywhere. So how do you enter this beautiful van to sit behind the steering wheel, to start the engine, to take off—perhaps even to pick up some hefty cargo?

This might have been going through the minds of those interested in purchasing a Dodge Deora, an amazing futuristic van from the designer Harry Bentley Bradley and brothers Mike and Larry Alexander. And why wouldn't they be interested? The car's so beautiful and elegant. Not for nothing did this pickup receive nine awards when presented in 1967 in a Detroit showroom! Back to the prospective buyers. So how did one get behind the wheel? By tipping the windshield and swiveling the lower gate. Awe-inspiring, surprising, and impractical. And what was that about a spacious body? Well, it was mostly taken up by the engine, cooler, and fuel tank. Looks can be deceiving. So let's ask ourselves—what's this pickup truck actually good for? For show? Definitely! To make work easier? Definitely not. So it's unsurprising nobody actually saw this extravagant gold doorless 1967 Dodge Deora pickup on the road. It never went into production. Of course, children could—and still can—drive it on the floor. That's because this marvelous truck inspired a Hot Wheels toy car. And all for the better. Such a beauty does deserve some love.

The original Dodge A100 Pickup

The original model
is notable for its doors,
which open from
the front. To get in,
you simply open
the windshield up
like a trunk.

M-497 TURBOJET TRAIN

The German Schienzenzeppelin (meaning rail zeppelin) was 37 years older and was fitted with a pusher propeller. A single prototype was made and was never put into operation.

"**W**e're taking off!" called the guards as the doors slammed shut and the trains left the stations, which were desperately half-empty.

In 1960s America, the car industry reigned supreme. If you didn't have your own car, you were a nobody. And if you needed to travel far away, you took a plane. Who would bump along in a slow old-fashioned train during such modern times? So, the 1960s began calling on the railways to change. And to change drastically!

Donald Wetzel, a U.S. marine and train engineer, racked his brains over this for so long that he got a truly groundbreaking idea—he'd fit the train with a bomber's jet engine. How bombastic! At a nearby air base, Wetzel spent a mere $5,000 on two jet engines from decommissioned planes, found a suitable wagon, and got busy. At first, he wanted to place the powerful jet engines on the roof, in the back of the wagon. But one night after dinner, his beloved wife Ruth thwarted his plan by taking a napkin and drawing a railway car boasting jet engines on the front part of its roof. Ruth's improved design promised to make the ride safer and faster, and so Donald Wetzel changed his mind and opted for his wife's solution.

On June 23, 1966, the M-497 Black Beetle speed-train set out for its first test journey, and it certainly didn't embarrass its creators. On the straight sections of the Ohio railway it managed an astonishing 184 miles per hour—an unimaginable speed up until then. Despite its stunning success, the Black Beetle didn't stay long on the track, allegedly because passengers found the exhaust gases rising from the jet engines too scary. So Don Wentzel used his jet engines to remove snow drifts from North American tracks. But don't be sad! The Black Beetle may have failed, but it opened the door to future high-speed trains, as it proved that both speed and safety were achievable on a modernized railway. And that's quite a feat in and of itself.

The engines were originally designed to supplement the Convair B-36 Peacemaker bomber.

EMA 1

Electric cars have long stopped being a siren song from the future and have turned into a common part of our daily lives. But did you know that the concept of the electric car is as old as that of combustion-engine vehicles? Back then, though, it seemed better and more profitable to put oil in cars instead of batteries, despite how bad car exhaust is for the planet. Over the past century, though, there have been several attempts at launching electric cars. One of the most notable ones concerned a small inconspicuous car from the former Czechoslovakia.

Today, the EMA 1 (short for Electric Municipal Automobile 1) can be seen in the Technical Museum in Brno, Czech Republic. If circumstances had been just a bit different, though, it could have been admired and driven on Czechoslovak roads, as well as throughout Europe and perhaps the whole world.

The car was designed by Brno engineers and in 1970 was introduced at the Man and the Automobile expo, where it overshadowed a similarly devised British Ford Comuta model. Both cars were supposed to present a solution to the budding oil crisis that was stoking fears of fuel shortages.

The EMA boasted a futuristic design, with large windows, thin frames, and ground-breaking technology, which was ahead of its time by a good decade.

But the Council for Mutual Economic Assistance crunched the numbers and decided to move the production from Czechoslovakia to Bulgaria, untroubled by the fact that Bulgaria had no experience making electric cars. The project ended before it started. In 1972, Czechoslovakia lost any hope of becoming a superpower in producing electric cars, the rise of which was delayed by another 50 years.

The second prototype of the EMA 1, with completely steel bodywork, was finished in 1970 and is exhibited in the Technical Museum in Brno, Czech Republic.

The first functional prototype, with makeshift bodywork and no doors, made in 1969.

CONCORDE VS. BOEING

The Concorde, a supersonic plane of British-French design, kept U.S. aircraft engineers up at night. What if the company were to take over aviation and send the American air industry packing? This scenario needed to be prevented at all costs. But how? By making a U.S. supersonic plane that'd be just as good, that's how. And so the search for the American "Concorde" began in the early 1960s.

Since the U.S. government was so invested in the project, it decided to largely fund it. Three companies participated in the prestigious tender—Boeing with its Boeing 2707 design, Lockheed with its L-2000 prototype, and North America Aviation with its NAC-60 model. The last one was soon excluded from the competition, as it had nothing on the other two, more ambitious designs. In the end, the more luxurious Boeing beat the simpler Lockheed, which lagged behind due to its significant performance requirements.

Compared to the Concorde, the Boeing 2707 was supposed to be larger, accommodate more passengers—nearly 300—and fly further, not only across the Atlantic but also across the Pacific to Asia. Sadly, the ambitious project soon ran into unsolvable issues related to its heavy fuselage. Additionally, the lighter material it was made with (titanium) was too expensive and wouldn't pay off. And the sonic booms caused by the plane flying at supersonic speeds were the final nail in the coffin. The United States had no other choice but to abandon their pursuit. Who knows what it would have been like, being able to choose between the supersonic U.S. Boeing or the European Concorde?

A model of the Boeing 2707 displayed in the Hiller Aviation Museum in California. It's 300 feet long, with a wing span of 180 feet.

A life-sized model
of the Lockheed L-2000
prototype.

MERCEDES-BENZ ESF 05

Anyone who's ever sat in a car knows to buckle their seatbelt. If there's an accident, it will keep you in your seat. Seatbelts have saved many lives, just like airbags that pop out of the dashboard when a car crashes hard. As the number of cars grows, unfortunately so does the number of accidents. Fortunately, though, modern vehicles are becoming safer and safer.

As a fun exercise, look at older models and pay attention to their windows, which are much larger when compared to the new ones, with thicker frames. But why are the windows smaller? For safety, of course! The

The ESF-05 model, with its elongated front, hydraulic shock absorbers, electric window openers, and five three-point seatbelts.

The rear, with sidelights and rear-controlled lights. The rear and front windshields were both made from glued, layered glass.

goal is to protect the car if it flips over. Then again, there haven't always been so many cars, and neither have they been so fast and large as they are today. Decades ago, you rarely saw more cars on the road than you could count on your fingers—that's how rare they were. And to boot, they weren't very fast. Way back when, a person with a flag would warn pedestrians that a motor vehicle was moving down the road. It's been over a hundred years since then, but at one point between our car-heavy era and the times when an automobile was viewed as an impossible invention by the French writer Jules Verne, engineers had to consider the safety aspect of the increasing numbers of cars.

During this time, Mercedes Benz introduced its ESF series, the undisputed pioneer in personal car safety. This test series, including the latest model, the ESF-2019, has been making traffic safer ever since. But you won't spot them on the road.

THE DALE CAR

The three-wheeled two-passenger Dale, designed by Dale Clift, was the flagship project of the Twentieth Century Motor Car Corporation.

After World War II, the world didn't worry much about the price of oil. Engineers designed cars with powerful engines for buyers to act like little boys and argue about whose four-wheeled darling had more horse power under its hood. But then 1973 came, and a huge shock came with it—OPEC (short for the Organization of the Petroleum Exporting Countries) decided to reduce oil production and start regulating oil prices. But the price of fuel skyrocketed. Manufacturers and fans of powerful cars had no idea what to do because their vehicles became too expensive to operate. And then an extravagant three-wheeled low-cost light car literally rushed in.

Its top speed was almost 85 miles per hour, and it could turn away from hitting a wall at 50 miles per hour with only a scratch. So said Elizabeth Carmichael, an enterprising woman who immediately took a liking to the design by Dale Clift and promised him the world if he would allow her to manage the production and development of a car that was so well suited for the oil crisis era. Allegedly, when this extraordinary vehicle underwent a stress test, it was operated by Carmichael herself.

As it turns out, though, her work on the project was a scam. The prototypes were immobile and the money went poof. And the swindled investors weren't the only ones with eyes popping out of their heads—the police who came to arrest the fraudster were surprised as well. Carmichael had managed to escape from her house just before they arrived, leaving behind only some wigs and dresses. The case made much more sense, though, when it was discovered that Elizabeth Carmichael had another identity—that of a wanted forger and fraudster named Jerry Dean Michael!

CITROËN KARIN

As we know, people love their cars and even give them nicknames: Pugs, Vee Dubs, Ronda, and many others. The sky's the limit! But perhaps only one car brand has a funny nickname as a part of its actual name: the 1980 Citroën Karin. Karin translates as *darling*, and this exceptionally atypical car definitely was the darling of its designer, Trevor Fior. Karin is sort of a glassy four-wheeled pyramid. The driver sits alone in the front, in the middle of the car—just like a pharaoh—while up to two passengers can settle themselves in the back. The car is dominated by a striking steering column. The top of the pyramid—sorry, the roof of the car—is miniature compared to other automobiles; it can fit only a single sheet of paper.

If you thought the car was being driven on highways all over the world by people who loved extravagance, you'd be wrong. The Darling wasn't meant for regular use and was never expected to go into serial production. Rushing down the highway while seated in a moving pyramid would definitely have caused quite a stir, right?

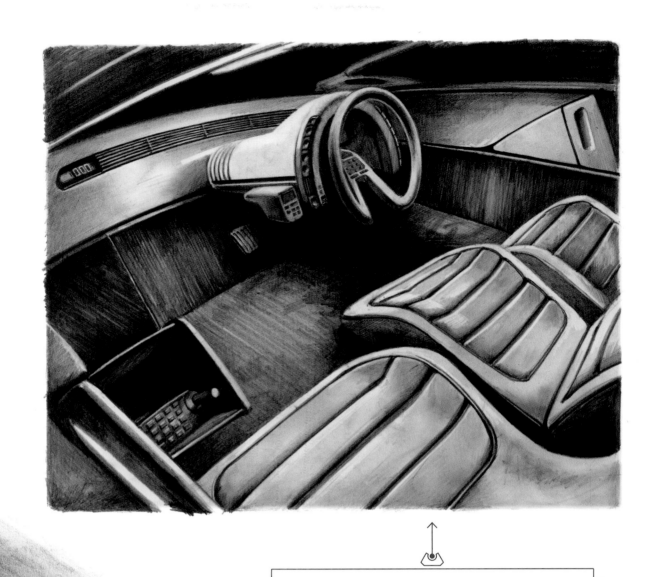

The unusual cabin layout is dominated by a row of seats for three passengers, with the driver sitting in the middle.

The design was introduced in 1980 at the Salon de l'Automobile, also known as the Paris Motor Show. Owing to the car's pyramid shape, the roof was as small as a sheet paper.

FOLDING SCOOTER

Hey, we're almost at our destination. The breeze wafting in the streets is caressing our cheeks. We're weaving our way between the cars stuck in traffic. But what is that? There's no parking spot around? No problem. We just get off our mini scooter, fold it up nice and small, turn it into a comfortable piece of roller luggage, and go to our appointment, never late and always on time.

No, this isn't a fever dream or a sci-fi story; it's reality. You're in 1980s Japan, where the world's smallest scooter went into production—the Honda Motocompo,

The Honda Motocompo could fit into the trunk of its Honda City and Honda Today models produced in the 1980s.

Honda Today

Honda City

a scooter that can confidently fit into a suitcase, as small as a toy. How ingenious!

But the 1980s weren't too kind to this groundbreaking invention. After two years and 54,000 of these wonderful folding Hondas being made, their production ended once and for all in 1983. Perhaps because this luggage, sized for a trunk, could be lifted only by the strongest of people, as it weighted a hefty 100 pounds. You'd work up quite a sweat as you shoved it into the trunk. Phew! And you'd better hope you have enough space to perform this storage ritual. Despite these obvious drawbacks, though, the Honda Motor Company has been thinking about reviving its cult 1980s folding suitcase, maybe this time for an electric scooter or an electric kick scooter.

LUN-CLASS EKRANOPLAN

It rested quietly on the seashore, its robust body striking fear in the hearts of those who saw it: the *Lun*-class ekranoplan. In the 1960s, Soviet engineers spared no effort to create these gigantic monsters, which were neither ships nor planes. The first of them, the mysterious Caspian Sea Monster—as it was known—was a monster indeed. So why did Rostislav Alexeyev design it?

So that the Soviets would be ready to fight aircraft carriers during the Cold War, that's why. The Caspian Sea Monster was a ground-effect vehicle capable of flying and floating just above the surface of the water by creating a pocket of air between the wings and the water. The ekranoplan—as the half-boat, half-plane hybrid heavy-duty machine was known—could fly directly above the water's surface, becoming virtually invisible to enemy radars. Undetected, its huge body could

The ekranoplan flew at a top speed of 340 mph.

transport missiles, mines, and all manners of weapons. The Caspian Sea Monster never truly succeeded, and after a fatal accident in 1980, it was left to sink. In 1987, the most famous ekranoplan premiered as the *Lun*-class ekranoplan. It remained in service until the late 1990s, but this promising giant met its predecessor's fate when it was buried under the sea after the whole project was canceled.

It wasn't recovered until decades later, in July 2020, when three tugboats and two additional vessels hauled it to the shore of the Caspian Sea, all the way to the Russian city of Derbent, where it was supposed to be displayed in public. But along the way it got stuck on a sandy beach, where it lay until the end of the year, like a whale washed ashore. Then it was finally moved to safety.

KINEO 27

It's a hot summer day. The air carries the scent of cakes cooling on the windowsill. The rustle of leaves mixes with the singing of birds. And you don't even mind that your bus is 15 minutes late. Why would you? It's a Sunday morning and you have lots of time.

Then all of a sudden, a sports car sweeps past you, passing two villages in a minute, ruining the peaceful morning with roaring and rumbling. It disappears as soon as it came. The sleepy day goes back to normal,

and all that's left of the experience is the burning smell of exhaust gases that'll be tickling your nose for quite a while.

This event will etch itself in your and the driver's memory as a meeting of two blurs, the only difference being that you at least heard the car while the driver likely didn't see you at all.

This story is like that of Horst Stross and his luxury Kineo boats. The Austrian businessman wanted one thing more than any other, and that was to make a Porsche Carrera 911 sports car traverse seas and oceans, dazzling the whole world—and perhaps also some unsuspecting sea creatures. There were several versions of the design, inspired by luxury sports cars and dolphin anatomy. The various-sized prototypes of this luxury vessel boasted not one but several sports engines. The size determined the number of engines, and thus how loud this means of transport would be. Which was one

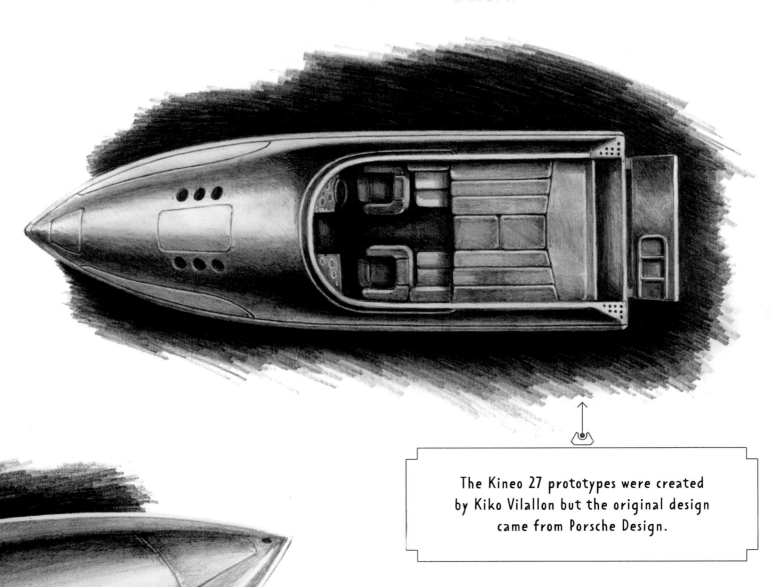

The Kineo 27 prototypes were created by Kiko Vilallon but the original design came from Porsche Design.

The boat's design was chiefly inspired by dolphins and the Porsche 911.

of the first, and sadly not last, issues the project ran into. Noise really isn't something you'd want your luxury pleasure boat to suffer from, no matter how fast it is. Uncomfortable deck use was another obstacle Stross's ambitious dream struggled with. Think about it—would you enjoy walking on the deck and admiring sea waves while your boat is speeding through the ocean?

And because the project was subject to constant changes, endless complications, and bold financial decisions, Horst Stross had no other choice but to give up on his dream. The smallest and best-known Kineo—the Kineo 27—was officially presented in 1993 in Düselldorf, but its creator had to admit that he himself couldn't even afford such a boat—it was six times as expensive as the Porsche 911! This exorbitant sum deterred all prospective buyers and the whole project became nothing but a story from the past.

NASA X-38

"**S**o long, safe journey, enjoy your stay. And if you run into any problems, don't worry! We'll send an emergency vessel to pick you up."

The U.S astronauts who were to serve on the International Space Station had nothing to fear. Their colleagues on the ground had developed a special rescue vessel—the X-38. The developers, engineers, and designers left nothing to chance. Since 1995, at the Johnson Space Center, they'd been carefully planning and building prototypes of the world's best emergency vessel available. In terms of technology, they naturally combined and tried everything to withstand the test of time.

In the end, they came up with the small X-38, which deployed a parachute during landing and fit easily into a space shuttle. It could accommodate seven astronauts and automatically transport them back to Earth if they were ill or injured and thus incapable of piloting the vehicle. The boat weighed 23,500 pounds, was 30 feet long, and was powered by an intricate system of batteries with a life of nine hours—triple what was needed to get the crew to safety. Sadly, this amazing project soon exceeded its budget, and for this reason, in 2002 it was canceled.

PEUGEOT MOOVIE

Any driver, whether they're experienced or a beginner, can confirm that a mini car is the best choice for urban traffic. The type of car is so tiny you can park it pretty much anywhere without driving around and around hoping to find a spot. In 2005, at the Frankfurt automotive fair, an exceptional and truly miniature vehicle was presented, one that was suitable even for the most crowded of cities. At 7.5 feet long, it was destined for urban streets. Its original and extravagant appearance, reminiscent of a glassy droplet moving on two large hollow wheels, impressed anyone who appreciated unusual designs. Moreover, both hollow wheels functioned as doors for entering the vehicle. Propelled by an environmentally friendly electric engine, this striking yet highly functional mini car amazed the 2004–2005 jury of the Peugeot design competition. So much so that they almost unanimously awarded it the first place. The designer, 23-year-old

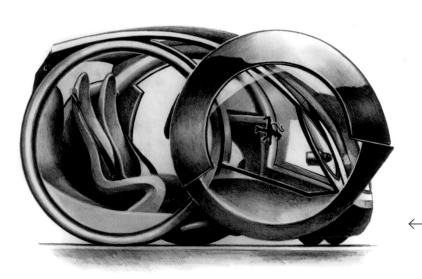

Unique car door opening

André Costa, had every right to be proud. Too bad
these tiny drops aren't riding around in the streets—
there'd be a lot to admire.

MEANS OF TRANSPORT
THAT *ALMOST* CHANGED
THE WORLD

© B4U Publishing for Albatros,
an imprint of Albatros Media Group, 2023
5. května 1746/22, Prague 4, Czech Republic
Written by Štěpánka Sekaninová & Tom Velčovský
Illustrated by Martin Sodomka
Translated by Radka Knotková
Edited by Scott Alexander Jones
Printed in China by Asia Pacific
www.albatrosbooks.com

ISBN: 978-80-00-06845-9

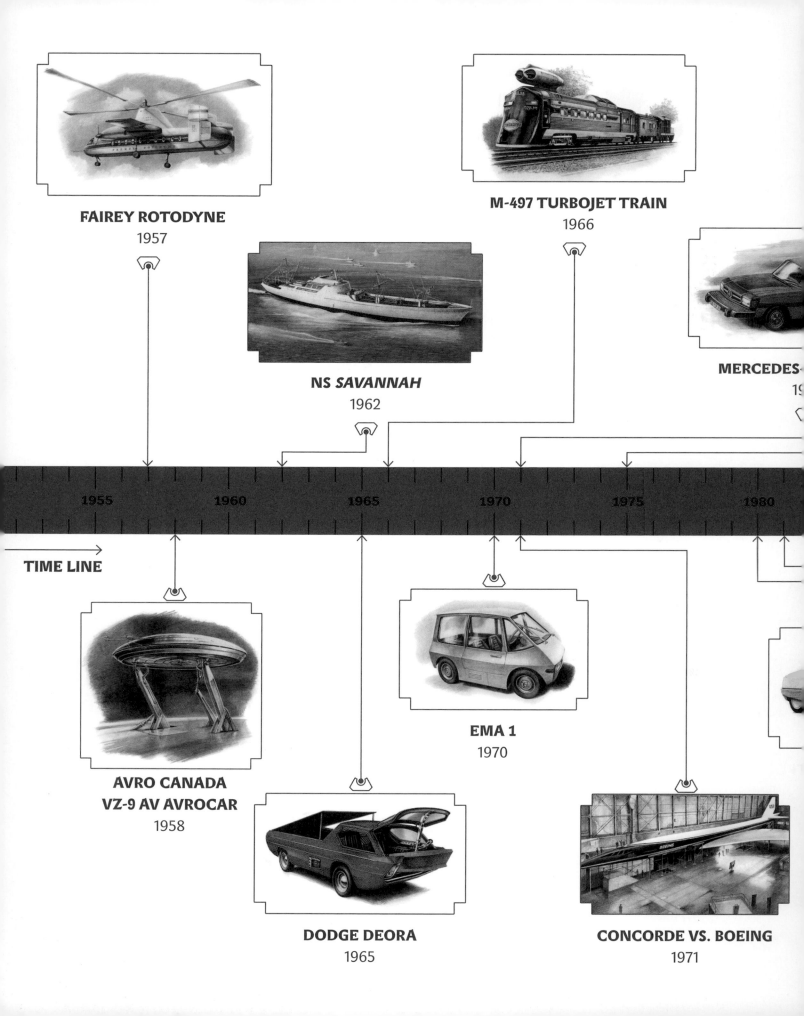

FAIREY ROTODYNE
1957

M-497 TURBOJET TRAIN
1966

NS *SAVANNAH*
1962

MERCEDES-
1

1955   1960   1965   1970   1975   1980

TIME LINE

**AVRO CANADA
VZ-9 AV AVROCAR**
1958

DODGE DEORA
1965

EMA 1
1970

CONCORDE VS. BOEING
1971